29 Tips for

Craft Fair Vendors

Brenda DeHaan

Jahva Bear Publishing
Printed in the USA

DeHaan, Brenda.
29 Tips for Craft Fair Vendors
   1. Crafts and hobbies. 2. Home-based businesses.
   3. Vendor displays. 4. Handicrafts. 5. Marketing.
   6. Entrepreneurship 7. Jewelry
   745.5

Contents

Business basics...aka the somewhat boring background preparations 5

Branding time 7

Think inside the box, outside the box...just reuse that box (or whatever).........................13

Ways to display 24

Marketing..48

Final tip...51

About the Author..52

Books by Brenda DeHaan 53

It is always handy to have a quick list of tips on what you need as a craft fair vendor from the basics to clever displays. If you are new to craft fairs, this list will be extra helpful. Being comfortable with multiple ways to prepare and arrange your displays is also an advantage.

In addition to covering the principles of setting up a craft fair booth, colorful photos from actual events illustrate the points. Even better, they may trigger a different approach for your own booth. You never know what could inspire a fresh idea for your handcrafted displays.

 These air plant holders resulted from a craft fair customer asking me if I could make an air plant holder with wire and a crystal. She'd seen some online. I hadn't heard of such a thing, looked on online for examples, and then created these three. My customer was so happy that she said she's going to buy more air plants and have me make more holders.

Crafters are creators, and ideas are our business!

Business basics...aka the somewhat boring background preparations

1. File any necessary paperwork to get your business sales tax ID information all situated. Search online for your state's Department of Revenue, and they can guide you from there.

2. Cash in with payment options (check, cyber cash and credit/debit card). Few people carry cash for larger purchases, so provide ways to pay digitally. You may want more than one electronic option. Technology glitches happen.

3. Experiment with the most efficient ways to pack and transport inventory.

How many trips does it take you to get your inventory inside?

Could you do anything differently to reduce your tips?

4. Take pictures or screenshots of each craft fair's details like set-up times. Before the customers arrive, take photos of your booth from a distance and close-up pictures. Create a craft fairs folder on your phone to store the photos in one handy album. Then it is easy to review what you need to do and remember certain displays for future shows.

My Albums

Craft fairs October...

This top album photo was from when I practiced a **Z** layout before my first show using it.

Branding time

5. What type of theme best reflects your product and personality? Examples include boho, natural neutrals, signature colors, chakra colors, black and white, traditional, geometric, refined, rustic, vintage, your favorite color, etc.

The brown kraft paper label reinforces the natural theme. Giving the soap its own name adds to the overall vibe.

The sage bundle and orgonite pyramid in chakra colors complement the chakra layout kits containing healing crystals in heart shapes.

The deer antler points to the hunting theme while displaying duck calls for sale.

6. Business cards promote future business. Your cards should complement your brand and products. If you order cards with information on only one side, you have space on the back to add more personal information or notes for specific customers or requests. Your cards can include QR codes to take people to your website, Etsy store, social media page, or wherever best markets your business. Depending on your product's size, your business card could double as your price tag.

7. Design a sign that fits the theme of your style and inventory. Many companies make custom signs for reasonable prices. Do you want a retractable vinyl banner that sits on a tabletop or the ground? Would you rather have a custom tablecloth with your business name? Whatever you prefer, the customer needs to be able to see your business name.

8. What color and type of table coverings will you use? Some are stretchy and tight, some are tailored for craft fairs and events with open backs and no hanging corners, and some are traditional tablecloths. Your tablecloth choices probably depend on whether you transport your own tables and know the exact sizes or if you use tables provided at the show.

   What color would make your inventory grab the customers' attention? Solid colors usually work the best, but a jacquard, ombre, or very subtle pattern might work as well. If you prefer patterns, they function best with a solid-colored runner on top with the pattern showing on the sides of the table.

You want contrasts because light-colored items are easier to see with a darker background while dark items benefit from light colors behind them. Taupe and similar neutral colors are adaptable where seasonal scarves, runners, or placemats can change their look.

Most vendors store items underneath their tables. Make sure that the tablecloth doesn't drag on the ground where customers (or you) could trip.

Some crafters roll their tablecloths between events to avoid wrinkles. Thicker fabrics or those with spandex or lots of polyester are less likely to wrinkle. Read the description details and reviews if you order online. One "wrinkle-free" tablecloth says in the fine print that it's wrinkle-free after ironing!

9. Your attire could continue your theme with a shirt designed with your logo on your banner, sign, or tablecloth. You could wear a signature color.

The banner and shirt were designed from a photo of the azurite with malachite necklace. Enlarged, it resembles the world.

Which of your creations would photograph well for a sign or banner to represent your business?

Think inside the box, outside the box...just reuse that box (or whatever), when possible!

10. Recycle or upcycle containers, especially for transporting inventory. Egg cartons, plastic ice cream containers, and metal chocolate containers are useful for packing jewelry, magnets, crystals, or other small items.

The heart-shaped containers work to display heart-shaped jewelry, rose quartz carved hearts, and other lovely products. Egg cartons work well for separating jewelry items.

A disadvantage of this chocolate container is that customers must be close to see inside. The advantages are that the bracelets transport easily and set up very quickly. Just remove the lid, add the price sign, and you're done.

From peppermint ice cream to serpentine eye masks, this oval container contains goodies. Then the masks' display reuses a vintage metal candy dish (or relish tray) with the handle folded out of the way.

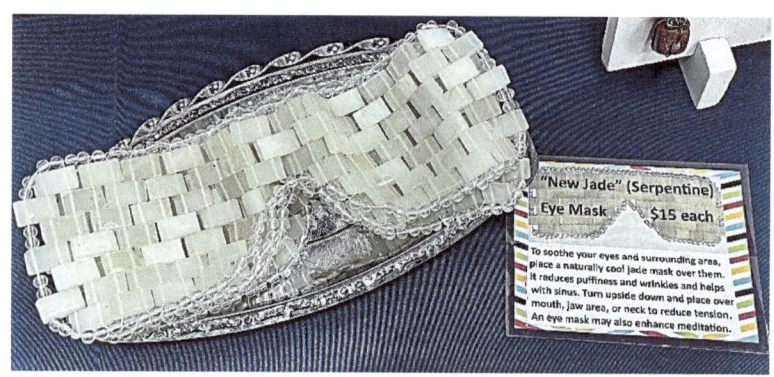

A folding room divider can also divide your space from your neighbor's booth while displaying wreaths or other items that benefit from a vertical display. A solid-colored background would work even better, but sometimes we just use what we have at the time and retain its original purpose back home.

Cupcake holders can be thrift store finds that work as displays to lift and feature a variety of products.

11. Vintage props are cheaper and add character. A rustic patina or an appeal to nostalgia trigger emotions that often induce sales.

This booth balances bushel baskets of gourmet popcorn. The vendor explained that the vintage baskets are sturdier and better overall than the newer ones they've tried.

12. Making DIY props can save you dollars to make more dollars. Then items can be just how you want.

This vendor's husband built a stand that does triple duty: transports items on casters, provides storage space, and creates a checkout station.

When this crafter needed multiple sturdy stands for her sun catchers, her husband made some for her. This type of stand would also work for wind chimes and necklaces.

Metal stands designed for wreaths also work for hanging sun catchers and mix well with the handcrafted wood stands.

13. Research online and in interesting stores for trends, product ideas, and other inspiration; then add your own creative twists. You want to be original, of course, but you also need to offer something that is in demand. Search for trends in different parts of the country for ideas that haven't become common in your area yet.

When I saw a chain with beads on a boot advertised on social media, I wanted something fun to decorate my shoes and created my own. I simplified from using a chain with two charms to one charm that easily threads through the laces and doesn't get dangled.

I put the shoe on a small stool on the outside edge of the table along the aisle to make people wonder why that shoe was there and investigate.

When I attended my cousin's wedding, I immediately noticed the wire flowers at each table setting. His bride has a bridal consulting business  and had created 200 wire flowers. The "wedding flower" party favors were all wire (like the bottom one), but I made my own version by adding a gemstone bead in the center and then wire-wrapping each flower to larger rough crystals for a one-of-a-kind home décor item.

 It's always fun debuting a new product at a craft fair! Have you thought about creating any new products to add to your inventory?

Ways to display

14. Experiment with table layouts. Booth sizes vary. Table sizes vary. Inventory amounts vary. You need various table designs in mind.

If the event provides tables, they are usually 6' or 8' long. Occasionally, they may have some round tables also. Although this circular shape can be tricky, with the right products and tiers, a table in the middle can set you apart.

With a new layout, set up a trial run in your living or dining room the night before with the main items. Then you will have everything out to pack and will be able to set up more quickly the next day. Remember to take pictures. Load your vehicle the night before the show with as much as feasible.

With one table, it will probably be used as a counter display along the aisle. Two tables can be utilized like the number **11** or letters **L** (regular or inverted), **V,** or **T**. With three, you may form a **Z** or **U**. I have never seen a **Y** formation, but "why" not try it sometime?

In case you're wondering, the **Z** formation is stylized where the middle table forms a straight line, not a diagonal. The three tables form zones where you may move easily between them. Play around with paper rectangles to see what will work the best.

Unless you have a corner or a large booth, shorter tables work better for your **Z**. They don't have to be the same size. Using 4', 5', or 6' tables give you space to maneuver. A common combo is two 6' tables placed horizontally and one 4' table vertically.

Whatever sizes you choose, place the longest table along the aisle for more visibility. People who might be hesitant to enter a booth are comfortable viewing the outer table and then may continue browsing at the vertical and back tables.

EXAMPLES WITH TWO 8' TABLES

This **V** design divided the jewelry from the books and crystals. The tray behind the banner was the pay station.

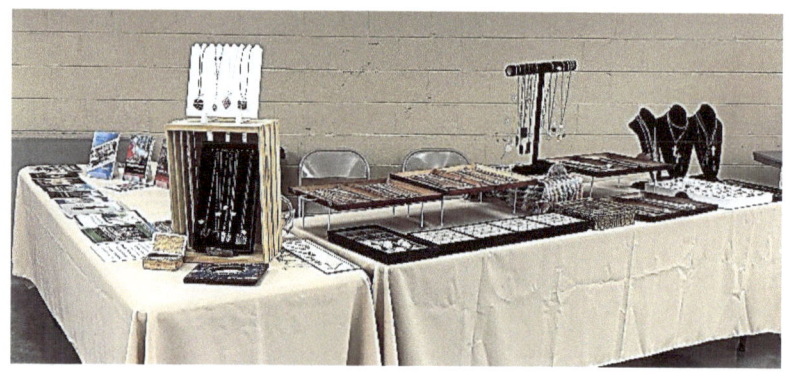

An **L**-shape is a standard design because it functions weLL. The layout gives you lots of space behind the tables to help customers.

The next layouts are just quick examples to experiment with options. The tables are marked 6' x 2', but the sizes can have other dimensions. Pictured are an **11,** inverted **L, U,** inverted **U,** and **Z.**

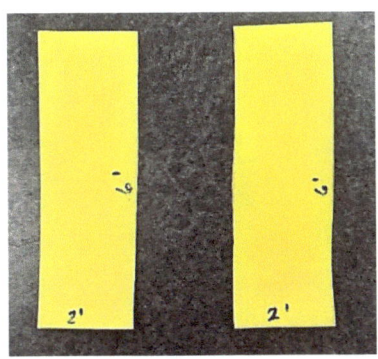 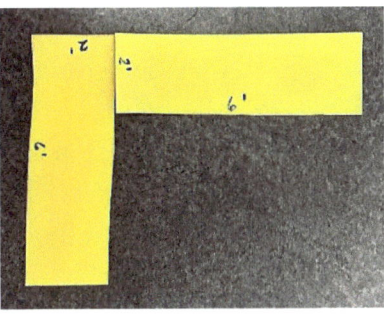

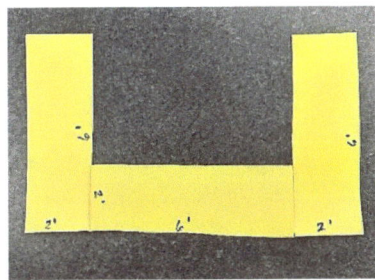 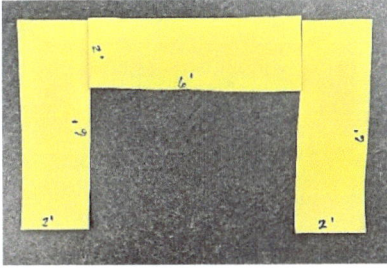

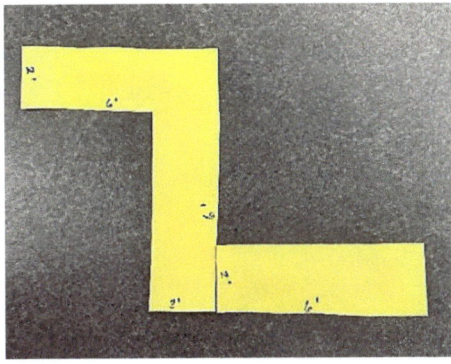

15. Employ more height for more sight. In other words, flat displays for flat sales; raise items for higher sales.

How many of these have you used?

- wood crates
- shelves
- wood step stools
- vintage ladder
- wire shelf organizers
- bookcases
- your storage tubs camouflaged under fabric
- benches (folding or solid)
- baskets
- grid walls
- room dividers
- pegboard cases or stands
- panels made from chicken wire and wood
- wire closet organizers (set up vertically with zip ties)
- display risers
- spice racks
- plant stands
- vintage suitcases
- easels
- A-frame shelf display
- clothing racks
- PVC pipe stands
- wire cubes
- coat tree

Placing the shelves along the back wall creates a backdrop; more importantly, it prevents the shelves and contents from being inadvertently bumped. If you don't have a wall, put it in the most solid, secure space.

A folding pegboard case adds height and convenience. Anything that saves time setting up is a win.

When items are small, strive to make them stand tall.

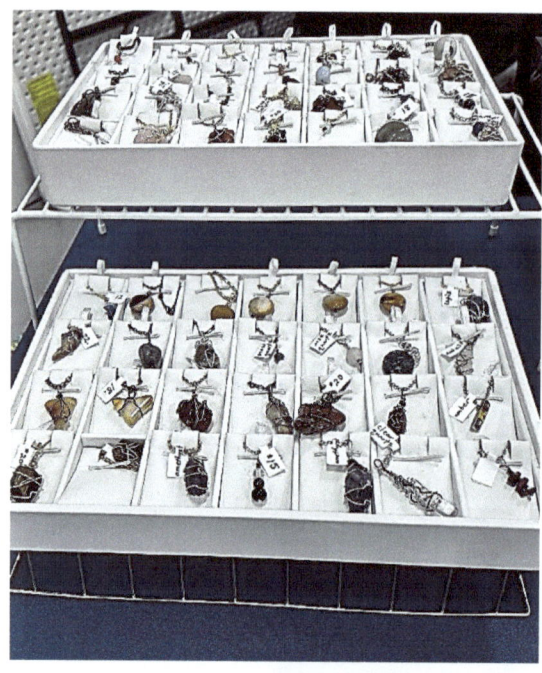

Lifting products enough to create layers adds that little touch to "up" your game.

Cover the line of shelf organizers with scarves or runners to create a linear lift.

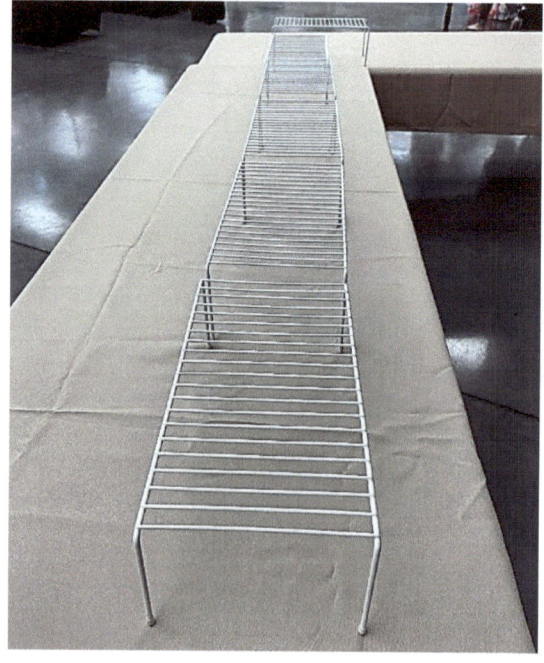

Use furniture risers under your tables. They are affordable and may hold over 1,200 pounds. The pictured set has 8 adjustable pieces to add 3"-8" of height, depending on the desired effect. (Only four are pictured to illustrate the options.)

- Risers add presence to your booth by raising your table physically and visually.

- Small children are less likely to "rearrange" your items on taller tables.

- Higher tables reduce back strain because you don't have to bend over as far.

Rise above the other booths!

16. Group items to create multiple areas of interest. You can group by color, similarities, style, function, size, etc. Groupings create cohesive arrangements for people to pause and focus.

Books are on one side of the table with jewelry on the other. The rocks are organized by colors and size on their own tray display.

A different view shows how groups of boxes and other groupings add interest.

Baskets are lightweight containers with neutral colors and pleasing textures. Serpentine ("new jade") and rose quartz facial rollers fit well in this basket. Many customers are unfamiliar with gemstone rollers, so they make a good conversation starter.

Carved gemstone angels are grouped by books about angels to continue the theme.

17. People appreciate patterns and balance in their viewing. Then they can focus better on what's being displayed instead of unconsciously seeking to determine how items were designed and displayed. Human brains like order and patterns.

This stair-step grid lifts items and showcases them.

The bamboo tray coordinates well with the wood necklace displays behind it.

18. Diversify with price points and products. Many shoppers have limited budgets but would still like to support the vendors. It's nice to have a few items for $5 or less.

I thought crystal keychains would interest people for $5 each. Sales didn't get going until after a girl said that she was going to put one on her backpack. When I started suggesting that possibility to people, the keychains sold.

The prices here range from $2-$5. Children who collect rocks can find something affordable, and it

reinforces how the wire-wrapped jewelry has been created with natural crystals.

19. Capture attention with an unexpected feature. It could be a surprising item placed somewhere unpredictable or a decorative vignette.

Author Kim Luke created dioramas from her children's book series at her book stand at Festival in the Park.
I loved them, and children gravitated to them.

Inspired by Kim Luke's dioramas, I added vignettes to my book displays, which paid off—literally! The fairy garden scene relates to some of my children's books.

The stuffed cat and miniature house now travel to craft shows with me to highlight my cat Apollo who jumps from our garage to house roofs and back daily. The rest of the time, my grandkids enjoy playing with him.

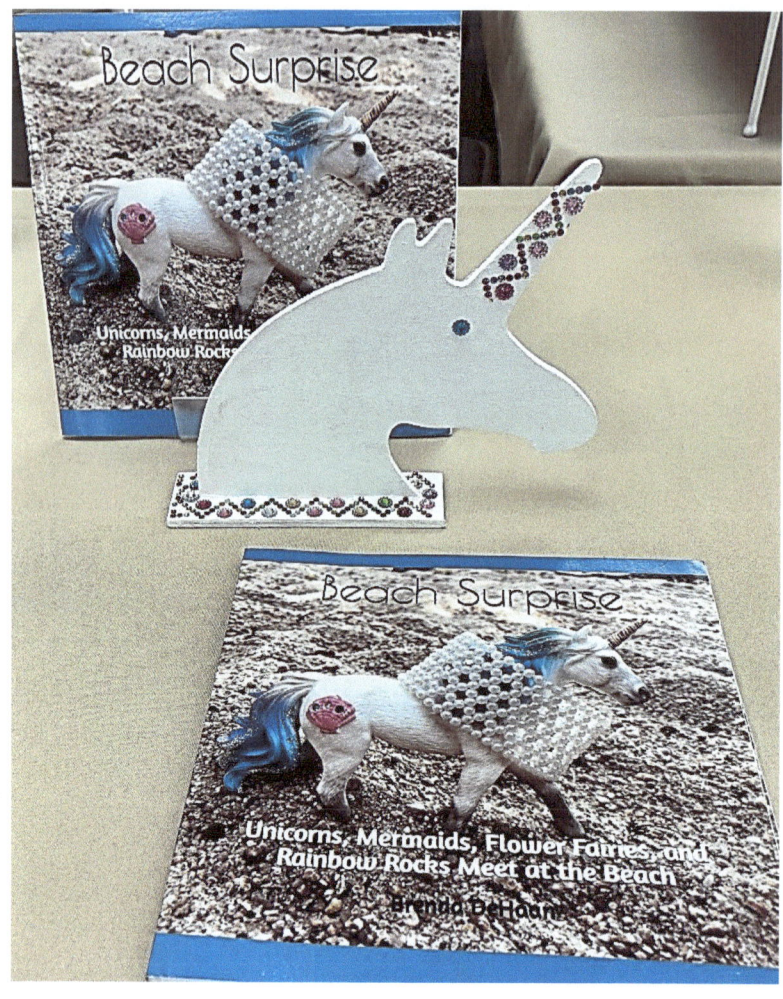

While looking at this display, a girl begged her grandma to buy her "the unicorn book." The grandma would not buy her a book. I was so tempted to just give the girl the book, but then others would have wanted free books.

This scene creates nostalgia and the desire to recreate those fond memories of playing with dolls and toys for someone else.

20. Plants and other elements from nature add a fresh appeal. At one show, the organizer bought mum plants on clearance and gave each vendor a plant to display and keep. It was a fun touch for everyone.

Some vendors use silk plants to add a "natural" look to their booths.

21. Have clear prices because many customers are uncomfortable asking. It's often, "No price, no purchase."

Notecards may be utilized as price signs for items that don't have to be individually priced. Print the descriptions and prices in black and white and use packaging tape to adhere the details to the card's front.

Marketing

22. Join social media groups to learn about area shows and to get support.

23. Self-promote online, on paper, and in person (This is no time for humility.) Create your own event and tag their sponsoring organization's event. If willing to do custom work, advertise that you will accept orders before the show and will bring them to the event if people will be there or will mail them if they won't be.

24. Make signs with subtle suggestions. "Grandma loves jewelry" plants the idea of buying a gift for Grandma.

25. Prepare general statements to greet customers as they enter your area. You want to welcome them but not dominate their attention away from your creations. "How's your day going?" "Did it ever warm up outside?" "Let me know if you have any questions." Acknowledge them, but then let them browse.

26. For edible products, samples of the goods' goodness tempt people into purchasing.

Samples help to narrow down which of the 50 flavors must go home with you. Taste buds are powerful recruiters!

27. Clear bags continue to clearly promote your creations as customers continue to shop. Other shoppers may see the items through the bag and ask where they had been purchased.

28. Show appreciation. Thank people for looking or buying and thank the event's organizers.

Final tip

29. You need to protect your own energy and health. Craft fairs make for long days (and nights) between preparing, setting up, visiting with people all day, dismantling your booth, loading your vehicle, unloading everything back home, and putting everything away.

Most of the time, you will be on your feet. You may want to buy an anti-fatigue mat if you'll be standing in the same spot a lot.

You definitely need quality shoes with good support. It's better to wear ugly, comfortable shoes with arch support than cute shoes that give you a backache and sore feet. Not many people will see or notice your feet, anyway.

Buy good shoes. You are worth the investment— and put some shoe charms on those expensive shoes!

About the Author

Brenda DeHaan is a wire-wrapper, writer, and librarian in two school districts. She spends a lot of time straightening books on shelves and straightening chains at craft fairs. She started wire-wrapping in November 2011 and has been selling at craft fairs since March 2012.

Please follow *Brenda DeHaan, author* on Amazon, Facebook, and Instagram.

Books Crafted by Brenda DeHaan

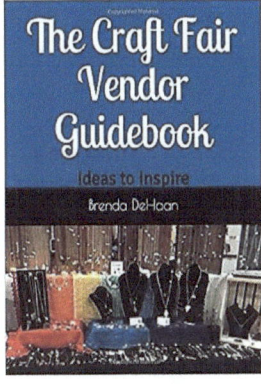

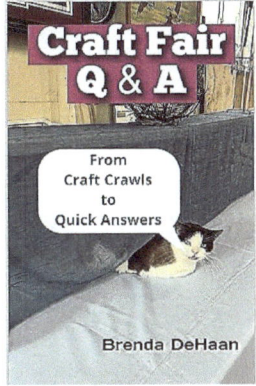

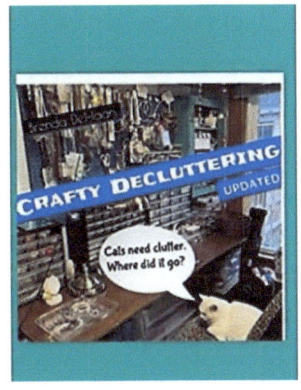

Children's Picture Books

Jasper Kitty Finds a Family

Jasper Kitty Gives Little Dog Jumping Lessons

Jasper Kitty Shares 17 Cat Tips

Jasper Kitty Gets a Brother

Jasper Kitty's Three Christmas Trees

Rocks Rock: Rough and Tumbled, Colorful and Cool Rocks and Minerals

ABC Amazing Book of Crystals

The Flower Fairies Meet the Talking Rainbow Rocks

Beach Surprise: Unicorns, Mermaids, Flower Fairies, and Rainbow Rocks Meet at the Beach

Crystals for Kids: Learn the Names of 17 Rocks and Minerals

Hooray for a Fun Day!

Rocks with Socks and Fox

Rocks and Rhyme 2 in 1 Fun: Crystals for Kids and Rocks with Socks and Fox

Adventures with Apollo: The Cat Who Rules Rooftops

Abenteuer mit Apollo

Cat Naps, Dog Naps: Who Naps More?

From Apple to Zombie Drawing Challenge: Illustrate Your Own Halloween Book

From Angel to Zzzz's Drawing Challenge: Illustrate Your Own Christmas Book

Tweens and Teens

Shine Life a Crystal: 12 Quick Tips to Rock Life
*Life Advice for Teens from an Ageless Grandma: Tips
and Encouragement Just for You*

Healing Crystals

*Rockin' Crystals: How Healing Crystals Can Rock
Your Life*
Crystal Haiku: Nature Poetry That ROCKS!
Crystal Angel Affirmations
Wie Kristallengel ermutigen
My Amethyst Journal
My Rose Quartz Journal
My Apache Tear Journal

Writing

*Self-Publishing Painlessly for Free: A What-to-Do
List for Frugal Authors*

Library Genrefication

*Where Are the Spooky Books? How to Genrefy Your
Library: Weeding, Moving, and Genrefying*

www.ingramcontent.com/pod-product-compliance
Lightning Source LLC
Chambersburg PA
CBHW050825290526
45792CB00001B/271